Opposites

Les contraires

leh con-*trair*

Illustrated by Clare Beaton

Illustré par Claire Beaton

B SMALL PUBLISHING

BILINGUAL BOOKS

big

grand

little

petit

p'tee

fat

gros

grow

thin

mince

hot

chaud

show

cold

froid

frwah

clean

propre

prop

dirty

sale

push

pousser

pooss-*eh*

pull

tirer

tee-*reh*

noisy

bruyant

brwee-*yoh*

quiet

tranquille

tron-*keel*

heavy

lourd

light

léger

leh-*sheh*

wet

mouillé

mwee-yeh

dry

sec

sek

happy

content

con-toh

sad

triste

empty

vide

veed

full

plein

plahn

long

long

long

short

court

koor

A simple guide to pronouncing the French words

Les contraires	leh con-*trair*	**Opposites**
grand / petit	grohn / p'tee	**big / small**
gros / mince	grow / manss	**fat / thin**
chaud / froid	show / frwah	**hot / cold**
propre / sale	prop / sal	**clean / dirty**
pousser / tirer	pooss-*eh* / tee-*reh*	**push / pull**
bruyant / tranquille	brwee-*yoh* / tron-*keel*	**noisy / quiet**
lourd / léger	loor / leh-*sheh*	**heavy / light**
mouillé / sec	mwee-*yeh* / sek	**wet / dry**
content / triste	con-*toh* / treest	**happy / sad**
vide / plein	veed / plahn	**empty / full**
long / court	long / koor	**long / short**

Published by b small publishing
Pinewood, 3a Coombe Ridings, Kingston-upon-Thames, Surrey KT2 7JT
© b small publishing, 1993
1 2 3 4 5
Design: *Lone Morton*
Editorial: *Catherine Bruzzone*
Colour reproduction : Shiny Offset Printing Co. Ltd., Hong Kong.
Printed in Hong Kong by Wing King Tong Co Ltd.

ISBN 1 874735 20 4 (paperback)
ISBN 1 874735 25 5 (hardback)
British Library Cataloguing-in-Publication Data.
A catalogue record for this book is available from the British Library.